YORUBA

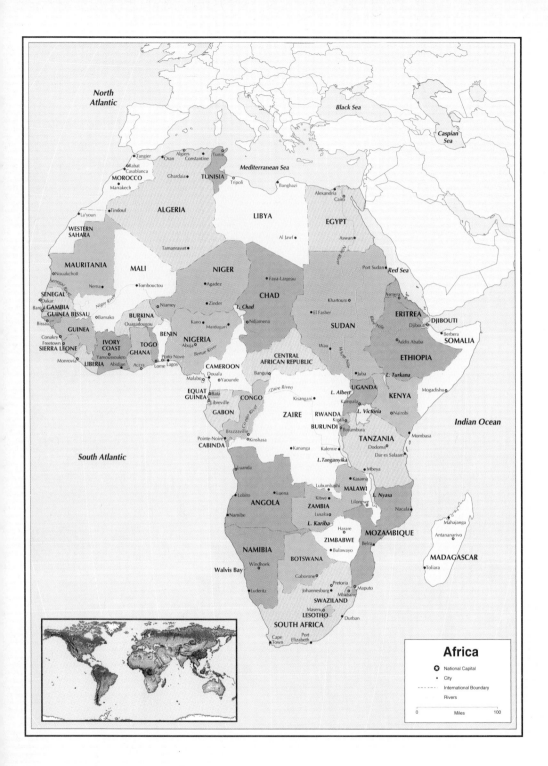

The Heritage Library of African Peoples

YORUBA

Michael O. Anda, Ph.D.

THE ROSEN PUBLISHING GROUP, INC.
NEW YORK

Published in 1996 by The Rosen Publishing Group, Inc.
29 East 21st Street, New York, NY 10010

First Edition

Manufactured in the United States of America

Library of Congress Cataloging-in-Publication Data

Anda, Michael O.
    Yoruba / Michael O. Anda. — 1st ed.
      p. cm. — (The heritage library of African peoples)
    Includes bibliographical references and index.
    ISBN 0-8239-1988-9
    1. Yoruba (African people)—Juvenile literature. I. Title.
II. Series.
DT515.45.Y67A53   1995
960′.0496333—dc20   95-15070
                                        CIP
                                        AC

Contents

INTRODUCTION

THERE IS EVERY REASON FOR US TO KNOW something about Africa and to understand its past and the way of life of its peoples. Africa is a rich continent that has for centuries provided the world with art, culture, labor, wealth, and natural resources. It has vast mineral deposits, fossil fuels, and commercial crops.

But perhaps most important is the fact that fossil evidence indicates that human beings originated in Africa. The earliest traces of human beings and their tools are almost two million years old. Their descendants have migrated throughout the world. To be human is to be of African descent.

The experiences of the peoples who stayed in Africa are as rich and as diverse as of those who established themselves elsewhere. This series of books describes their environment, their modes of subsistence, their relationships, and their customs and beliefs. The books present the variety of languages, histories, cultures, and religions that are to be found on the African continent. They demonstrate the historical linkages between African peoples and the way contemporary Africa has been affected by European colonial rule.

Africa is large, complex, and diverse. It encompasses an area of more than 11,700,000

square miles. The United States, Europe, and India could fit easily into it. The sheer size is an indication of the continent's great variety in geography, terrain, climate, flora, fauna, peoples, languages, and cultures.

Much of contemporary Africa has been shaped by European colonial rule, industrialization, urbanization, and the demands of a world economic system. For more than seventy years, large regions of Africa were ruled by Great Britain, France, Belgium, Portugal, and Spain. African peoples from various ethnic, linguistic, and cultural backgrounds were brought together to form colonial states.

For decades Africans struggled to gain their independence. It was not until after World War II that the colonial territories became independent African states. Today, almost all of Africa is ruled by Africans. Large numbers of Africans live in modern cities. Rural Africa is also being transformed, and yet its people still engage in many of their customs and beliefs.

Contemporary circumstances and natural events have not always been kind to ordinary Africans. Today, however, new popular social movements and technological innovations pose great promise for future development.

George C. Bond, Ph.D., Director
Institute of African Studies
Columbia University, New York

Yoruba culture has spread to many parts of the Americas, particularly Brazil, Cuba, and the Caribbean. This woman in Brazil is a priestess of Shango, God of Thunder and Lightning. She carries double-headed axes and wears red and white, both symbols of Shango.

chapter

1

THE PEOPLE

THE YORUBA LIVE MAINLY IN SOUTHWESTERN Nigeria, but are also found farther west in the Popular Republic of Benin. They are one of the largest African ethnic groups, numbering 19 million in 1991.

During the four centuries of the transatlantic slave trade, about 1.5 million Yoruba were taken to the Americas, where their cultural and religious influence was—and still is—very strong. This spreading of Yoruba culture in Cuba, Brazil, the Caribbean, and parts of the United States is called the diaspora. Yoruba language, religion, art, myths, oral literature, music, dance, and cooking continue in the Americas, often with changes and dynamic adaptations to the new environment.

Yoruba culture from Africa and the diaspora

has become world famous, partially because of the wide variety and great beauty of its religious art. Today there are over 4,000 books and articles on Yoruba culture. In addition, several contemporary Yoruba have made significant contributions to world culture. Two outstanding figures are Wole Soyinka, Africa's first winner of the Nobel Prize for Literature, and King Sunny Adé, the famous Nigerian musician.

The name "Yoruba" was originally given to the Oyo Yoruba by their neighbors, the Hausa-Fulani. In fact the Yoruba consist of numerous subgroups and referred to themselves by these subgroup names, such as Oyo, Owo, Ketu, Ijebu, Shabe (Ishabe, Shave), and Ifonyin in Nigeria; and the Ana (Ife), Isha, and Idasha (Dassa) in the Popular Republic of Benin. The Yoruba language varies so much that a person from Owo may have difficulty understanding one from Ketu, but there is enough linguistic and cultural similarity to consider the Yoruba as a single but diverse group. However, among Yoruba groups in Africa and the diaspora there are many variations in language, spelling, names of deities, and other cultural matters.

The Yoruba are among the most urban of all African people. Today, the three largest Nigerian cities are in Yorubaland: Lagos (1,060,848); Ibadan (847,000); and Ogbomosho (432,000). This history of Yoruba urbanism goes back to

about the 11th century, when sacred rulers, who could be male or female, governed large city-states with the help of councils of elders. Some of the most important Yoruba kingdoms were Ife, Oyo, Owo, Ketu, and Ijebu. The various Yoruba subgroups seldom united in times of war and often fought against each other with the help of non-Yoruba allies.

▼ THE LAND ▼

The rhythm of farm work varies with the seasons, which consist of a dry season from December through February and a rainy season from April through October. The heaviest rainfall is in June, July, and September. Humidity diminishes as one goes inland. Rainfall averages between 40 and 80 inches. The temperature averages about 70 degrees.

Along the coast are swamp forests, behind which lie the rain forest, the savanna forests, and grasslands. Yoruba country is low-lying, about 1,600 feet above sea level. It extends inland to the River Niger to the city of Old Oyo, which was deserted in the 19th century. Several important rivers flow southward, emptying into the lagoon, which is separated from the ocean by a narrow and almost continuous sand bar. The lagoon system runs from the Popular Republic of Benin eastward to the Benin River, where it connects with the creeks of the Niger Delta. It

The Yoruba people are among the most urban in Africa. This is a view of the wharf in Lagos, where many Yoruba live.

The Yoruba are also rural farmers. These women are carrying gourds to market.

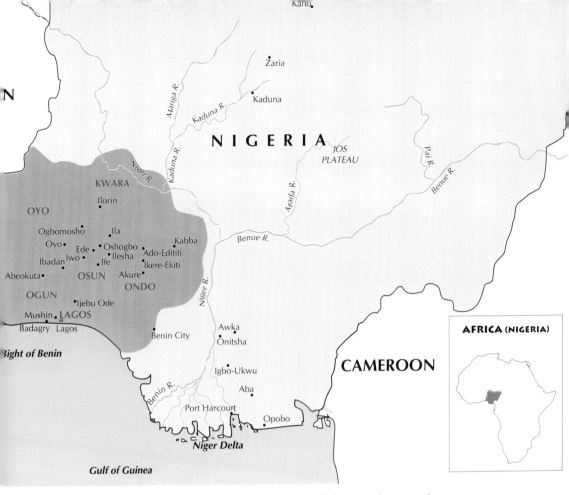

Map of Nigeria showing the location of the Yoruba people.

provides an inland waterway for small craft and an east-west trade route. The Ijebu Yoruba kingdoms (1400–1900), which flourished on this coastal trade, were the first Yoruba peoples to encounter Europeans in the late 1400s.▲

13

2
ORIGINS AND HISTORY

THE YORUBA ACCOUNT OF THEIR ORIGIN STATES
that the Yoruba originated in the city of Ife,
where the earth and the first human beings were
created. According to one version of this myth,
the deities originally lived in the sky, below
which there was only primeval water. The Creator, Olodumare, gave to Oshanla/Obatala, the
God of Whiteness and Creativity, an iron chain,
some earth in a snail shell or calabash, a five-
toed chicken, and a chameleon and told him to
climb down the chain and create the earth.

As Oshanla approached the gate of heaven he
saw some deities having a party; they offered
him palm wine and he drank too much and fell
asleep, intoxicated. Oduduwa, his younger
brother, had overheard Olodumare's instructions. When he saw Oshanla sleeping, he took

YORUBA PROVERBS

You know whom you love; you cannot know who loves you.

Youths who find fault with elders will one day be old themselves.

It is overindulgence that corrupts a rich man's offspring.

Do not marry early so as to have a lasting married life;

marry in haste and have a short married life.

Relatives-in-law should always be given a place of honor in one's estimation.

If one does not marry another person's daughter, one would not have to worship another person's deity.

When an old person cannot find a seat, something will prompt a young person to vacate his seat.

the materials and went to the edge of heaven, where he let down the chain and climbed down.

Oduduwa threw the piece of earth on the water, and placed the five-toed chicken upon it. The chicken began to scratch the earth, spreading it in all directions. Oduduwa sent the chameleon out to test its firmness before he stepped on it and made his home there.

Chief Yeyelorisa Olu-Ijio, a priestess of Obatala in Ife.

This myth does not really settle the question of Yoruba origins but rather explains many elements of Yoruba custom and belief. For instance, it explains why Oshanla forbade palm wine to his worshipers. It also explains the meaning of the full name of Ife (Ile-Ife) as Earth Spreading.

Ife and the surrounding area are the source of a number of extremely fine sculptures in terracotta, stone, and brass dating from 950 to 1400 AD. Many are very realistic human heads with decorative features that strongly

The Nok culture is an early Nigerian civilization that is probably linked both with Ife and with contemporary Yoruba culture. This terracotta head from northern Nigeria is thought to date from between 500 BC and 200 AD.

suggest that they come from early Yoruba civilization at Ife. This may be confirmed by the Yoruba myth of origin saying that Ife is the place where Yoruba culture began, and by the fact that the line of Ife kings remains unbroken from that time until today.

Many older sculptures, including human heads, have been found in the area of Nigeria where the Niger and Benue rivers meet. Dating from around two thousand years ago, it is likely that this early Nigerian civilization called Nok had a strong influence on later Nigerian peoples.

The Yoruba creation myth gives the Yoruba people a sense of unity through a common origin, since all claim descent from Oduduwa. Yoruba kings base their right to rule by claiming to be descended from him through one of his sixteen sons.

Archaeological digs at Ife have uncovered many beautiful sculptures. This bronze is a portrait of an Oni wearing a crown, beaded collar, and expensive trade beads of the kind still worn in Nigeria today.

Yoruba kings (obas) wear beaded crowns such as this one worn by Oba Jimoh Adebisi Okunade of Obaagun in Oshun State, Nigeria.

Today, there are more than fifty Yoruba kings who claim to be descendants of Oduduwa and to have migrated directly from Ife. There are more than a hundred kings in all. Some additional kings were granted the right to wear beaded crowns by other Yoruba kings, some kings took advantage of political unrest to declare themselves kings, and others did so under Pax Britannica, a peace imposed by Great Britain in the 19th century. Formerly, if a town chief (Bale) were to wear a beaded crown without the permission of the king (Oba) to whom he was subject, it was considered an act of treason.

▼ THE YORUBA-DAHOMEY WARS, 1698–1892 ▼

Recorded Yoruba history begins in 1698 when Oyo's cavalry invaded the kingdom of Allada in the south of what is now the Popular Republic of Benin. By this time the wars between rival kingdoms that fed the slave trade were well under way. Yoruba slaves were already being exported from the city of Whydah. Oyo, the largest and most powerful of the Yoruba kingdoms, defeated the Fon in 1724 and 1728, and as a result the King of Dahomey, now also part of the Popular Republic of Benin, began to pay annual tribute to the Alafin, King of Oyo.

In 1789, Dahomey attacked the capital of the Yoruba kingdom of Ketu, killing many and seizing captives. With some interruptions, which brought the Oyo armies repeatedly into Dahomey, the Fon tribute to Oyo was continued until 1827, when the King of Dahomey seized the opportunity to end the payments while the Oyo were at war with the Ilorin kingdom.

As the Yoruba kingdoms increasingly fought each other, Dahomean slave raids were frequently directed at Yoruba towns and cities. People old enough to remember these wars spoke with respect of the bravery and ferocity of the Dahomean women warriors who formed part of their army. The wars with Dahomey did not end until its armies were defeated by French forces in 1892.

▼ THE INTERNAL WARS, 1817–1893 ▼

In the late 1700s Oyo was enjoying the long, peaceful, prosperous rule of King Alafin Abiodun. But the Fulani, who had moved into Nigeria from the west as peaceful nomadic herders, began a *jihad* (a Muslim religious war) against their neighbors. From 1804 to 1810 the Fulani conquered first the Hausa, then the Nupe, the neighbors of the Yoruba to the north.

Meanwhile, the leader of Ilorin, Afonja, broke away from Oyo and invited bands of Fulani and Hausa warriors to Ilorin. They were joined by Hausa slaves who had revolted and escaped from Oyo. Together they raided nearby Yoruba towns and sold their captives into slavery.

The rule of Ilorin passed to Abdul Salami, the first of Ilorin's dynasty of Fulani Emirs. Oyo unsuccessfully attacked Ilorin several times. Finally, Old Oyo was deserted, probably in 1839, and the capital moved to Ago Oja, the new Oyo.

Meanwhile the Ife and Ijebu, together with Oyo refugees, destroyed Owu, a large, fortified town, after a siege of more than five years. They pursued Owu survivors into Egba territory, destroying Egba villages, and around 1829 they encamped in Ibadan. The Egba refugees moved south to found the city of Abeokuta in 1830, where they were joined by refugees from Owu. The Oyo in Ibadan built it into a gigantic armed

camp, which became the major force in the ensuing wars. When Ilorin besieged Oshogbo, in the early 1840s, the Ibadan army came to the rescue and the Ilorin army was decisively defeated, breaking its power but not ending its attacks on other Yoruba towns.

Other Oyo refugees settled in Ife, living in compounds scattered throughout the town and paying fees for the use of farmland. Shortly before his death in 1849, the Oni Abeweila assigned them land to build their homes at Modakeke, a site within the town walls of Ife. War eventually broke out between Ife and Modakeke. Ife was defeated, and its inhabitants fled seven miles south to Ishoya, where they remained until 1854. By this time, guns were increasingly available, and the Yoruba states fought costly wars with each other that continued to the end of the century. Ilorin conquered Ekiti and attacked other Yoruba areas in the northeast. Ibadan reconquered Ekiti and conquered Ilesha, fought in the south with the Egba, and raided for slaves among the distant Yagba and Bunu as well as within the Oyo kingdom itself. In 1862 Ibadan destroyed the large Oyo city of Ijaye. The Egba, who were still defending themselves against repeated attacks from Dahomey, became involved in a succession of wars with Ibadan, Ijebu, Egbado, and Awori.

These wars culminated in a sixteen-year war,

from 1877 to 1893, in which many of the Yoruba subgroups were involved in battles with Ibadan, which had only the support of Oyo.

▼ THE POSTWAR PERIOD, 1893–1960 ▼

The century of warfare left deep effects on Yorubaland. Political boundaries were redrawn to conform with the situation when peace was made, thus changing the size and shape of Yoruba kingdoms. This placed the Yoruba in Ilorin and Kabba Provinces in Northern Nigeria, whereas Ketu, Shabe, and other western Yoruba groups came under French and German control. Ife and Ilesha were placed in Oyo Province. Ibadan became an independent state. The former kingdom of Owu was destroyed, many towns and villages were obliterated, and large areas were heavily depopulated. Refugees settled among different Yoruba subgroups, creating a degree of ethnic diversity on a subgroup level that increased steadily with the greater mobility that followed the establishment of the Pax Britannica. The sixteen-year war left the Yoruba exhausted and willing to accept the British Protectorate, except for the Ilorin.

With peace established, European influences brought new changes to the old way of life. In 1900, the railway reached Ibadan. In 1904, the first bicycle reached Ife, causing some commotion. In 1907, the first Nigerian penny reached

Ife. In 1909, Modakeke, which at the time was two or three times the size of Ife, was dispersed. Some of its inhabitants went to farms in the direction of Ibadan, and others went to live on their farms around Ife. In 1914, the first District Officer arrived, and in 1918, paper money was introduced at Ife. In 1922, the people of Modakeke were given permission to resettle in their former site. Sir Adesoji Aderemi Atobatele became Oni in 1930. Following Nigeria's independence in 1960, he became the first Governor of the Western Region of Nigeria.

▼ BRITISH CONTROL, 1851–1960 ▼

The British, who had succeeded the Portuguese and the Dutch as masters of the slave trade to the Americas, had a change of heart and conscience. In 1808 they prohibited slaves from being carried on a British ship or landing in a British colony. They also assigned a naval squadron to patrol the Guinea Coast in an attempt to stop the traffic in human beings. When this measure met with only limited success, they attempted to make treaties with African kings to stop the slave trade. Interested in developing other kinds of trade with West Africa, the British soon established a colony at Lagos, a major port city.

In 1884–1893, the former Eastern Region of Nigeria was a Protectorate of Britain; it was joined with the Western Region and the Protec-

torate of Northern Nigeria on January 1, 1900, to form the Southern Nigerian Protectorate. On January 1, 1914, the two protectorates and the colony of Lagos were merged to form the Colony and Protectorate of Nigeria.

In 1960 Nigeria became independent. The first president was Dr. Nnamdi Azikiwe, who had led the struggle for independence. Soon Nigeria encountered political problems because of its large size and ethnic and religious differences. Politicians, corruption, and other factors created tensions. Christianized Yoruba and Igbo minorities in the south resented political domination by the Muslim majority in the north. The Hausa in the north resented the many educated Igbo who were appointed by the British to posts in the north, and in 1966 they murdered thousands of Igbo. The Igbo declared themselves independent of Nigeria, forming the state of Biafra. Nigeria declared war. When Biafra surrendered in 1970, 1.5 million Biafrans had died, many of starvation.

Such tensions and corruption continue to trouble Nigeria. Numerous military coups and fraudulent elections have prevented democratic rule.▲

chapter

3

RELIGION

The Yoruba universe is filled with spirit or life force, called *ase*, which comes from the creator, Oludumare. It is found in all living things, in rocks, in rivers, in spirits, deities, and ancestors, and in songs, conversations, prayers, and curses. *Ase* is flexible; it can be used for good or bad. Similarly, the numerous Yoruba deities, *orisa*, can be good or evil. In the middle of such competing forces, humans try to live out their destinies as best they can. They consult a diviner, the *babalawo*, to communicate with the spirit world of the *orisa* and the ancestors to find out what course of action will be advantageous and what sacrifices are required.

▼ MULTIPLE SOULS AND DESTINY ▼
Each individual is believed to have at least

two souls. The most important, the ancestral
guardian soul, is associated with the head, destiny, and belief in reincarnation. The second,
the breath, resides in the lungs and chest and
has nostrils to serve it. The breath gives people
life. A third soul, the shadow, has no function
during life. One can see the shadow and hear
and feel the breath, but no one hears, feels, or
sees the ancestral guardian soul while the person
is alive. However, the ancestral guardian must
occasionally be fed through sacrifices. At death,
the multiple souls return to heaven until the
ancestral guardian soul is born again.

A person is usually reborn into his own clan,
so that the guardian soul is often that of a
patrilineal ancestor. The names "Father Returns" (Babatunde) and "Mother Returns"
(Yetunde) are given to children of the same gender as the reincarnated ancestor. The identity of
the reincarnated ancestor is determined through
physical resemblances, similarities in character
or behavior, dreams, or divination.

Before a child is born or reborn, it is believed, the ancestral guardian soul appears before Olodumare (the Creator) to receive a new
body and breath and choose its destiny for its
new life on earth. Destiny involves a fixed day
upon which the souls must return to heaven; it
involves the individual's personality, occupation,
and luck. The day of one's death can never be

postponed, although other aspects of one's destiny may be changed by human acts and by superhuman forces.

▼ THE AFTERWORLD ▼

If a person has lived his full life span, his multiple souls proceed to the afterworld. Those who die prematurely remain on earth as ghosts. They go to distant towns where they are not known and settle there as traders. They may marry and have children. One may even marry a ghost without knowing it. If someone the ghost knew before death comes to town, it disappears. When the day appointed by Olodumare arrives, the ghost "dies" a second death and goes to heaven.

When the three souls reach heaven, the ancestral guardian soul accounts for all the good and bad deeds on earth. If a man has been good on earth, his souls are sent to the "good heaven" (*orun rere*). If he has been cruel and guilty of murder or theft, he is condemned to the "bad heaven" (*orun buburu, orun buruku*).

In the good heaven or "heaven of breezes" (*orun afefe*) life goes on as it does on earth. In the bad heaven or "heaven of potsherds" (*orun apadi*) the cruel people are beaten and made to walk in the hot midday sun. Suicides, like cruel people, can never be reincarnated. They become evil spirits and cling to the treetops like bats.

▼ THE DEITIES ▼

The Yoruba believe in many deities—some say over 200. Certain deities are worshiped throughout Yorubaland and have their counterparts among neighboring peoples and in the diaspora; others are of only local significance. Some important deities like Shango and Obatala are believed to have lived on earth where, instead of dying, they became gods.

Many deities are identified with a particular clan, in which case all members are worshipers. As a child usually worships the deity of his father's religion, so the child of a convert to Christianity or Islam generally follows his father's new religion. Many Yoruba and people of Yoruba descent blend Yoruba and other religions. The Afro-Cuban religion of Santeria, practiced in many parts of the Americas, identifies characteristics of Yoruba deities with Christian saints.

Those who are claimed by a deity are usually initiated as devotees through ceremonies that once lasted several months but have been shortened to a few weeks. They are secluded in the shrine, where they are taught the formalities of worship, and finally their heads are shaved and the deity possesses them, taking control of the body. Some deities, like Ifa, never possess. Shango possesses each initiate after his or her head has been shaven, but at his annual festivals

YORUBA DEITIES

The diaspora of Yoruba peoples that occured due to slavery spread Yoruba culture to many parts of the Americas and Caribbean. Although many elements of culture were changed in the new environments, Yoruba roots can still be seen clearly; as in this comparison of deities' names.

Deity	Nigeria/ Benin	Brazil	Cuba
creativity	Obatálá	Obatala	Obatalá
divination	Orunmila	Orunmila	Orula
epidemic, smallpox	Obaluaiye,	Omo-Olu	Babalu Ayé, Omo-Olú
gods of	Oshanlá	Oxala	Ochanlá
creativity	Oshagiyan	Oxaguiam	Ocha Guiña
and justice	Oshalufon	Oxalufom	Ocha Lufón
	Orisha Oko	Orixa Oko	Oricha Oko
healing	Osanyin	Osanyin	Osain
messenger	Eshù-Elégba	Exu	Echú. Eleguá
mother of smallpox	Nana Bukúu	Nana	Nana Buruku
ocean	Yemoja	Yemanjá	Yemayá
rainbow	Oshumare	Oxumare	Ochumare
supreme god	Olodumare	Olodumare	Olodumare
sea	Olókùn	Olokun	Olokun
sweet water, love	Oshun	Oxum	Oehún
thunder, lightning	Shangó	Xango	Changó
twins	ibéji	ibeji, mabasa	ibeyi
war, iron	Ogún	Ogum	Ogún
whirlwind	Oya	Oya Yansan	Oya Yansá

only one individual in a given group of worshipers is possessed. Other deities, like Yemoja and Oshun, can possess dozens of worshipers at the same time during their annual festivals.

▼ OLODUMARE, THE CREATOR ▼

Olodumare (also known as Olorun) is the God of the Skies and has been combined with the Christian God and the Muslim Allah. He is the father and creator of all other deities and stands above them. Unlike other deities, he has no group of devotees and no shrines. Nevertheless, he intervenes in affairs on earth and assigns and controls individual destinies.

▼ IFA DIVINATION ▼

Ifa is the name of the Yoruba divination system, and of the god who rules it. Like other religious literatures such as the Christian Bible or the Muslim Koran, Ifa consists of numerous verses. The verses combine stories of events, moral and practical instructions, and pieces of wisdom. The *babalawo* knows all the verses by heart. When visited for spiritual advice, the diviner casts a set of sixteen palm nuts or a special divination chain several times. Like the throws of dice, many combinations can result. The *babalawo* marks the outcomes into the chalk spread on his divination tray, and this becomes the sign that refers to the verses he is required

Yoruba diviners play a crucial role in Yoruba religion. This *babalawo* wears the white robes typical of his profession. Whiteness symbolizes the purity and calm that are required to communicate effectively with the spiritual world.

to recite for the client. The verse will also suggest a course of action and the appropriate sacrifice.

Ifa, the God of Divination, also called Orunmila, is a scholar and scribe who organized and recorded all the knowledge and wisdom in the Ifa verses.

Olodumare gave Ifa the power to speak for the gods and communicate with human beings through divination. Whatever personal deities they may worship, all believers in Yoruba religion turn to Ifa in time of trouble.

Orunmila is associated with the colors green and yellow combined, or blue and tan.

▼ ESHU: THE DIVINE MESSENGER ▼

Eshu, or Eshu-Elegba, carries sacrifices from humans to the *orisha*, and brings rewards and

Eshu, the messenger of the Yoruba deities, has many art forms associated with him. These beaded figures, made this century, represent Eshu.

punishments from the *orisha* to humans. He is thus essential to the functioning of Yoruba religion and Ifa divination, and this is why his face often appears in a prominent place on the *babalawo's* divination tray— as if he were the overseer of the divination process.

Eshu is also known as the trickster, for he loves to play tricks on both humans and the gods. He is a master of disguise and of opposites. He likes to paint one side of his face black and the other white, so that people watching him from opposite sides will afterward argue about what they saw when he passed.

Although he can cause many confusions and reversals of fortune, nothing in religious practice can be achieved without Eshu's cooperation. Eshu is said to reward his many followers with

There are specific priests and shrines for each god. Pictured here is a Shango priest. He also appears to be a devotee of Ogun.

This is a shrine dedicated to the god Shango.

great wealth. He is also called Prince of Cowries, because cowrie shells were once a form of currency among the Yoruba and Eshu is associated with wealth.

▼ OSHANLA, THE GOD OF CREATIVITY ▼

Oshanla is the deity of creativity and justice. His name means "God of the White Cloth" (*Orisha ala*); his association with whiteness suggests the qualities of calm, purity, and justice. He made the first human forms, and he sculpts all human beings even before they are born.

▼ OGUN, THE GOD OF IRON ▼

Ogun, the patron of all those who use iron tools, including blacksmiths, woodcarvers, leather workers, barbers, locomotive and automobile drivers, hunters and warriors, is also the God of War.

▼ SHANGO, THE GOD OF THUNDER ▼

Shango is the God of Thunder and Lightning. Zigzag patterns, a symbol of lightning, are a sign of Shango. He hurls thunderstones to earth, killing those who offend him or setting their houses on fire. Some say Shango succeeded his father Oranmiyan as one of the early kings of Oyo.

▼ GODDESSES OF WATER ▼

Olokun is Goddess of the Sea, and her

In Yoruba religion the color white is associated with calm and purity. It is worn by many priests and priestesses, such as Omolajaye Olroke seen here in a shrine in Ife dedicated to the deity Obaluwaye who protects against distress.

Unlike "hot" dieties such as Shango, many female deities are "cool," including Yemoja, a goddess of the waters. Seen here is Helena Gomes Barbosa dos Santos, a priestess of Yemoja in Brazil where the diety is called Iemanjá.

daughter, Yemoja, is associated with water generally, particularly with the ocean, streams, and the River Ogun. One Yoruba story states that Yemoja, a large and fertile woman with many children, left her husband after he ridiculed her. Carrying a container that Olokun had given her, she stumbled and smashed it. The container turned into the River Ogun, and Yemoja became a stream. Her husband changed himself into a mountain and blocked the stream. Yemoja called to Shango, who blasted a hole through the mountain, allowing Yemoja to flow to the sea and rule the waters. Yemoja is associated with the colors blue and white combined, with crockery and porcelain containers, and with stones worn smooth by the action of water. Oshun is the Goddess of Love and Sweet Water. She is associated with the color and substances of brass and honey, and also with porcelain.

These three goddesses have many devotees in West Africa, Brazil, Cuba, the United States, and other parts of the Americas. They are generally benevolent and "cool," compared to the hot-tempered Shango and other aggressive and harsh male *orisha* such as Ogun and Obaluaiye, the God of Epidemics. But male gods like Obatala can be "cool," and female deities can be "hot"—like Shango's wife Oya, who is Goddess of the Whirlwind.▲

chapter

4

YORUBA SOCIETY

▼ *IDILE*: THE CLAN ▼

Every Yoruba is born into a patrilineal clan
(*idile*) whose members are descended from a
common male ancestor and are regarded as
blood relatives. Whereas the children of a man's
son belong to his clan, those of his daughter
belong to the clan of her husband.

Marriage with a clan member is strongly prohibited. Marriage is patrilocal, meaning that the
bride generally lives in the compound of the
groom's father.

The clan is thus a grouping whose male
members generally live together until death, and
whose female members live with them until
marriage. The clan is a corporate group, owning
its compound, the farmland outside of town,
and intangible property such as titles to political
and religious offices. It includes the dead (who

may be reborn into the clan) as well as the living. Its members are stratified by seniority, gender, and achieved status.

The clan is headed by its eldest male member, known as the Bale or "father of the house" (*baba ile*), a term that also refers to the head of a family. The eldest male clan member of the compound is always its Bale. An incompetent Bale retains his title even if another elder is appointed to perform his functions. The Bale presides over disputes. A husband is responsible for settling quarrels within his family.

Hierarchy within the clan is based on seniority and is important in regulating conduct between members. Each person is "elder" (*agba*) to all others born or married into the clan after him.

In seniority or age, the male clan members of the compound are divided into three groups: the elders (*agba ile*), the adult males who are economically independent (*isogan*), and the young men and boys who are economically dependent on their fathers and who are referred to as "children of the house" (*omo ile*).

Reciprocal obligations involve authority on the one hand and deference and respect on the other. Males are seated and served according to seniority, and elders can take better portions of what is served. This right, to which juniors cannot object, is termed "cheating" (*ireje*). Similar rights are associated with political office.

▼ THE FAMILY ▼

The clan and the subclan are more important than the immediate family comprising a husband, his several wives, and children. This is partially because the immediate family is relatively unstable compared to the permanence of the clan. Husbands and wives may divorce, but one's blood relatives never change.

When a father dies, his personal property is divided equally between the eldest male children of each wife. Each takes one share in the name of all the children of his mother. He may keep and use this heritage as he sees fit, but he is held responsible for the economic welfare of the others. In any dispute a person will, in the words of a proverb, "take his mother's side" against his father's other wives.

▼ THE CHILD ▼

In Yoruba custom, when a child is born it is sprinkled with water to make it cry. No word is spoken until it does, to prevent it from becoming impotent or barren. The child is held by the feet and given three shakes to make it strong and brave, so that it will not be afraid of noises, and so that it will not experience spasms. The child is bathed and rubbed with oil. The mother is present at the bathing if she is able, but she must not speak until the bath has been completed. Only women attend the birth, but a male

Yoruba children are encouraged to learn their parents' trades. This young boy is laying out the warp threads for weaving.

doctor may be called in if there are difficulties. It is believed that delivery would be delayed if the husband were present. No one younger than the mother should be present.

The mother and child remain in the house for a period, usually six days for infant girls and eight days for boys. On the day the child is named, it is taken out of the house for the first time. The child is bathed. The mother bathes, dresses in fine clothes, and sits with her child near a bowl of water. The father comes forward and drops money into the water, announcing his name for the child. The mother names the child without contributing any money. Then the father's relatives, followed by others, drop small amounts of money into the water, each suggesting whatever name they like for the child.

▼ TWINS ▼

The Yoruba have the highest rate of twin births in the world. This appears to have been true for a long time, because important historical and religious figures like Shango are said to have had many twins. Shango, also called Lord of Twins, is associated with many items that are twinned or doubled, such as the double-headed axe that is one of his special symbols. Many patterns used in Yoruba art are significant in part because they are created by doubling pat-

tern motifs or elements. The juxtaposition of red and white is usually a sign for Shango.

Perhaps the best known Yoruba art is the tradition of carving wooden figures of twins, called *ibeji*. Twins are regarded as sacred beings who, if well cared for, will attract further blessings from heaven for the family. If one or both twins die, as often happens in premature births, a mother commissions miniature wooden statues as memorials, which she honors, feeds, and decorates. Many *ibeji* are covered with red camwood powder and have indigo rubbed into their coiffures, precious substances favored by the gods. Today some mothers choose to use photographs of twins or plastic dolls as the basis for memorials of twin children who have died.

A first-born twin, who is considered younger because he was sent ahead by the other, is called Taiwo, meaning that he came to inspect the world for the senior twin, called Kehinde, meaning that he arrived afterward. There are special names for the first, second, third, and fourth children born after twins, and also for children born with the umbilical cord around their neck, for children born face down, and for other circumstances of birth.

▼ MARRIAGE ▼

Girls were generally betrothed before puberty in former times. Sometimes they were promised

to a friend of the father's before birth. Usually, a man negotiated through an intermediary, while the girl's parents made inquiries into the suitor's character. With increasing mobility and more children attending school and college, couples now often marry without the traditional parental consent. If the suitor is approved, the engagement is sealed with gifts and the suitor's agreement to pay bridewealth.

Now, as in earlier times, the payment of bridewealth does *not* mean that women are purchased. They can own property and sue for divorce. Bridewealth creates a link between the two families. It encourages marital stability, because if divorce occurs and the woman is at fault, the bridewealth must be returned; if the man is at fault he cannot collect back what he paid. Finally, bridewealth establishes the husband as the legal father of the wife's children, regardless of the biological father.

During the present century, Islamic and Christian marriages have been performed. Christian marriages are sometimes unpopular since, by law, they must be monogamous. If all previous wives are not relinquished or if subsequent wives are married, the husband can be sued and fined.

When a man dies, his widows may become the wives of his younger brothers. A son can also take a widow of his father as his wife, unless she

Gelede is a women's society concerned with the market, ensuring the fairness of the king, and controlling antisocial behavior, especially of women. These are *gelede* masked dancers from Meko, Nigeria.

is his own mother. The bonds established between clans through marriage and bridewealth are thus not ended by the death of the husband, and heirs are responsible for the welfare of widows. Yet a woman can, if she desires, return to her own family or take a new husband if the bridewealth is refunded.

▼ DEATH AND BURIAL ▼

A child who dies is considered to be an *abiku*, one born only in order to die, and is buried immediately without being bathed, shaved, or dressed. In earlier times, all childless persons

were also buried in this way, but since 1920 childless persons older than twenty are buried in the house and a funeral feast is held in their honor. In Yoruba society, such funeral ceremonies can be attended only by guests younger than the deceased.

Elders' funerals have hundreds of younger guests, and a festive mood predominates. One should celebrate an elder who has had many children and has lived to a ripe old age. It is the duty of the heirs to perform the funeral properly so that the ancestor will be reborn and his soul will not trouble his descendants.

Annual Egungun festivals celebrate ancestors. Egungun masqueraders wear elaborate cloth masks and costumes composed of many layers of expensive fabrics. The spirits of ancestors enter the costumes and possess the dancers.▲

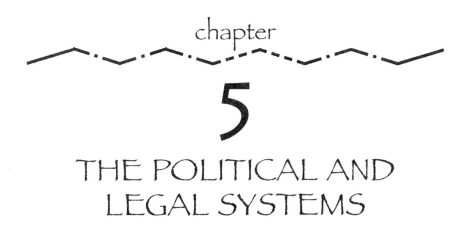

chapter

5

THE POLITICAL AND LEGAL SYSTEMS

BECAUSE THE YORUBA ARE SO DIVERSE, IT IS not possible to generalize for every Yoruba kingdom. However, the political system of Ife, where most Yoruba believe the world began and which was probably the center from which Yoruba civilization spread, provides an interesting example of Yoruba political and legal systems.

Before the wars of the 19th century, Ife, or more properly Ile-Ife, was the capital of a kingdom of moderate size, about 70 miles long and 40 miles wide. Its king, the Oni, ruled over the capital through his town chiefs and over the outlying towns through the Ife town and palace chiefs, the five provincial chiefs, and the local town chiefs (Bale). Although provincial chiefs were subject to the Oni, they had jurisdiction over internal affairs as long as they remained loyal.

Traditional Yoruba administration was carried out by many chiefs associated with the Oba, or king. Seen here is Chief S.F. Omisakin, holder of the administrative title Obalufe in Ife.

Ife itself is divided into five wards (*adugbo*), each comprising a number of precincts. Each precinct includes several compounds each headed by the eldest male clan member. The compounds are large, complex, rectangular structures, housing up to several hundred inhabitants. Formerly, they had windowless mud walls and gabled roofs thatched with broad leaves. Newer houses, however, have wooden shutters or glass windows, cement or brick walls, and corrugated metal roofs.

▼ THE KINGS ▼

Yoruba kings are considered divine. Because

they are considered direct descendants of Oduduwa, they cannot be deposed for strictly political reasons. In the past, when a king's rule was unpopular, mobs demonstrated outside the palace walls. The chiefs met and informed the king that the people rejected him. When this happened the king was expected to open a "calabash of death" containing a powerful charm, the sight of which killed him.

The king's person was sacred. Following the crowning of a new Oni of Ife, he moved into the palace and could return home to visit his relatives only in disguise and under the cover of darkness. He appeared in public only once a year, at the major sacrifice to Ogun. It was not until 1925, on the occasion of the visit of the British Prince of Wales, that Yoruba kings first met each other at Ibadan. The Alake of Abeokuta visited England in 1904 and 1937, following which several Yoruba kings made visits abroad. By 1937, the Oni appeared in public almost daily without his face being veiled. The Oni is chosen from the royal patrilineal clan, the largest clan in Ife.

▼ THE LEGAL SYSTEM ▼

Minor disputes can be settled by elders, instead of holding a formal hearing at the chiefs' courts, which involves a fee, calling witnesses, and the imposition of penalties or punishment.

John Adetoyese 'Leye I, Timi of Ede, in his palace courtyard.

A pair of bronze staffs used by the Ogboni Society, a judicial organization of Yoruba elders. The male figure on the left holds a miniature staff, and the female on the right gives the special Ogboni greeting of placing the left fist over the right with both thumbs hidden.

Oaths (*imule*) and ordeals (*aje*) are employed to determine guilt when the evidence is contradictory. A plaintiff may be made to swear by Ogun, touching his tongue to an iron object while asking to die if he is not telling the truth. Oaths by Ogun are recognized in the courts as equivalent to swearing on the Koran or the Bible.

In former times, disputes that could not be settled within the clan could be referred to the palace chiefs, who met daily outside the palace gate and jointly with the town chiefs every fourth day (*ojo Oja Ife*). If the matter involved members of Ife clans, the town chiefs were summoned immediately. Their decision was referred

51

to the Oni for his approval, or if no decision could be reached, another hearing was held in front of the Oni. It included the town and palace chiefs and other members of the Ogboni Society of male and female elders concerned with judicial matters.

Ogboni, called Oshugbo in Ijebu, also perform important political and religious functions. Only these highly respected elders can select and install the king, force him to abdicate, and bury him. Such great power in the hands of elders, even over the sacred king, shows the importance of elders in Yoruba society. The men and women of Ogboni form part of a political system of checks and balances that prevents everyone, including the king, from abusing sacred or earthly power and from breaking the law.

Native Administration Courts were established in the larger towns after 1912, and British criminal law was introduced, but civil law is still based largely on Yoruba customary law. Magistrates preside over higher courts. The authority of the Oni, his chiefs, Ogboni, and other aspects of the Yoruba legal system were weakened by the right of appeal either to higher courts or directly to the colonial District Officer.▲

6

THE ECONOMY

RURAL YORUBA LIFE IS CHARACTERIZED BY hoe cultivation, craft specialization, and trade. Hunting, fishing, animal husbandry, and gathering wild foods are widely practiced. Yoruba diet consists of starchy tubers, grains, and plantains, supplemented by vegetable oils, wild and cultivated fruits, vegetables, meat, and fish. Yams are the staple food in Ife. Although rice is grown in Abeokuta Province, cassava is the staple. North of the rain forest, sorghum and bulrush millet are important in the diet. Cocoa is the principal cash crop.

Poultry such as chickens, guinea fowl, pigeons, ducks, and turkeys are kept, and farm animals such as goats, sheep, pigs, cattle, and horses. Dogs, cats, rabbits, and guinea pigs are domestic animals. Wild birds and game are hunted. Fish and shrimp are caught in the

Cocoa is Nigeria's third largest export. The Michael Ige family remove cocoa beans from the pods on their family farm in Adamo, Nigeria.

ocean. Professional hunters and fishermen sell their catch fresh through traders in the market or dry it for sale in areas where fish and game are less plentiful. With the increasing population and expansion of cocoa-farming, large game has virtually disappeared in parts of the rain forest.

Palm oil is used in preparing stews that may be served alongside starchy dishes. The oil palm is also a source of palm wine. Wine is also made from the bamboo or raffia palm. Beer is brewed from maize and sorghum and, to a lesser extent, from bananas and sugarcane. Kola nuts, which serve as a stimulant, are traditionally offered to guests and are an important item of trade into Nigeria's interior. Cotton, indigo, tobacco, and gourds are also grown.

Farming is considered men's work in Yorubaland, although a few women work with their husbands or farm alone. A farmer usually works alone or with unmarried sons. But several men who have farms near each other may agree to a labor exchange. Alternatively, depending on the size of the task, a man invites his relatives, friends, and members of his club to form a working bee. The host provides food and drink for the group at the end of the day's work, but this is not considered payment. No strict accounting is kept of an individual's participation. However, if someone calls for working bees without taking part when others hold them, it is noticed and others will fail to respond to the invitation.

▼ CRAFTS SPECIALIZATION AND TRADE ▼

Nearly all rural Yoruba men engage in farming, but the production of many other goods is specialized. Weaving, dyeing, ironworking, brasscasting, woodcarving, calabash-carving, beadworking, leatherworking, and pottery, as well as hunting, fishing, drumming, diving, and the compounding of charms and medicines are occupations that have been mastered by small groups of professionals. More recently, sawyers, carpenters, brick makers, bricklayers, tailors, bicycle repairmen, automobile mechanics, shopkeepers, letter writers, and other professions have been added to the rural economy.

Craft specialization also meant the development of markets for the exchange of local produce. Markets are dominated by women traders, the principal exception being the men who butcher and sell cattle from the north. Women thus frequently have their own incomes and are often wealthier than their husbands.

▼ CURRENCY ▼

In the past goods were bartered, or cowrie shells were the basis of trade. Cowries were found in the coastal lagoon, but by 1522 they were being imported from the Malabar Coast

and, during the 1600s, from the East Indies. This resulted in their steady depreciation. Around 1850 the value of 2,000 cowries was four shillings sixpence. It soon fell to less than two shillings when cheaper cowries were imported from Zanzibar on the coast of East Africa.

▼ THE NATIONAL ECONOMY ▼

In the 1970s Nigeria was a rich country, producing 2.5 million barrels of a oil a day. Staggering sums were stolen by corrupt officials at every level of government. The democratic government of President Shagari, between 1979 and 1983, tried to stop corruption. Investigators sent to state departments, such as the national telephone company, found the records burned by arsonists destroying evidence of their frauds. A drop in the oil price and mass migration from the poor rural areas to the cities, where it seemed money could be made easily, contributed to a military coup in 1983 led by Major General Buhari. He too failed to stop corruption and improve the economy. Lagos became so large and full of crime that it seemed ungovernable. Many Nigerians became human "mules" who swallowed drugs wrapped in plastic to smuggle to other countries. Seeing little future in Nigeria, Nigerians began to emigrate in large numbers.

In 1985 Major General Ibrahim Babangida took over in a bloodless coup, determined to save the economy and return Nigeria to democratic rule. Unfortunately, the oil price dropped by more than 50 percent and Nigeria was unable to pay its debts. The government consulted experts on rescuing the economy and finding a democratic solution for the complexities of Nigeria. To harmonize religious and ethnic differences and reduce corruption, Babangida decided to allow only two political parties. Despite these efforts and the military's war against nepotism, corruption, and crime, life has become increasingly difficult for most Nigerians, who struggle to survive through subsistence farming in the rural areas.

In 1993 Babangida established a council for overseeing the transition to democracy. Within months, General Sani Abacha took over the council, abolished the government, and delayed the transition to democratic civilian rule.▲

Glossary

agba One who is older and therefore senior to another.

aje Ordeal or test to prove guilt or innocence.

Alake The king of Abeokuta.

ase Life force.

baba ile The male head of a clan.

babalawo Diviner and priest.

Bale A town chief; the head of an extended family group.

bee A group of workers.

ibeji Carvings of twins.

idile Patrilineal clan.

imule Oath; promise to tell the truth.

isogan Economically independent males.

jihad Holy war.

Oba A Yomba king.

Ogboni Elders.

ome ile Economically dependent males.

Oni The king of Ife.

orisa Deities.

polygyny Practice of having more than one wife.

For Further Reading

Aboyade, B. Olabimpe. *Yoruba Culture and Civilization: An Introductory Bibliography (1845–1976)*. Ibadan, Nigeria: Fountain Publications, 1991.

Areje, Raphael Adekunle. *Yoruba Proverbs*. Ibadan, Nigeria: Daystar Press, 1985.

Atanda, J. A. *An Introduction to Yoruba History*. Ibadan, Nigeria: Ibadan University Press, 1980.

Drewal, Henry. *Yoruba: Nine Centuries of African Art and Thought*. New York: Center for African Art in association with H. N. Abrams, 1989.

Galembo, Phyllis. *Divine Inspiration: From Benin to Bahia*. Albuquerque, New Mexico: University of Wisconsin Press, 1993.

Imoagene, Oshomha. *Know Your Country Series: Handbooks of Nigeria's Major Culture Areas*. Ibadan, Nigeria: New-Era Publishers, 1990.

Thompson, Robert Faris. *Flash of the Spirit: African and Afro-American Art and Philosophy.* New York: Random House, 1983.

Tutuola, Amos. *Yoruba Folktales.* Ibadan, Nigeria: Ibadan University Press, 1986.

Index

ABOUT THE AUTHOR
Dr. Michael O. Anda received his B.Sc. from the University of Lagos, and his M.A. and Ph.D. from the University of Wisconsin, all in Political Science. He has worked as a teaching assistant, an instructor, a lecturer, and an assistant professor at the University of Wisconsin.

Dr. Anda has been a member of the African Studies Association, the American Political Science Association, and the International Studies Association, among others.

Dr. Anda is currently an Assistant Professor of Political Science at the University of Arkansas at Little Rock.

COMMISSIONING EDITOR
Chukwuma Azuonye, Ph.D.

CONSULTING EDITOR
Gary N. Van Wyk, Ph.D.

PHOTO CREDITS
Cover by Herbert M. Cole; p. 12 Top © AP/Wide World Photos; pp. 12 Bottom, 41, 45, 50, 54 by Eliot Elisofon/ National Museum of African Art, Eliot Elisofon Photograph Archives, Smithsonian Institution; p. 17 © Werner Forman Archive/Art Resource NY, National Museum, Jos, Nigeria; p. 18 © Werner Forman Archive/Art Resource NY, Museum of the Ife Antiquities, Ife, Nigeria; p. 33 © Werner Forman Archive/Art Resource NY, Anspach Collection New York; p. 51 © Werner Forman Archive/Art Resource NY, Phillip Goldman Collection, London; pp. 8, 16, 19, 32, 34, 36, 48 © Phyllis Galembo.

DESIGN
Kim Sonsky

ADDITIONAL RESEARCH
Jonathan Zilberg